Dietmar W. Brandt

Hidden Toscana

Secrets of Lunigiana

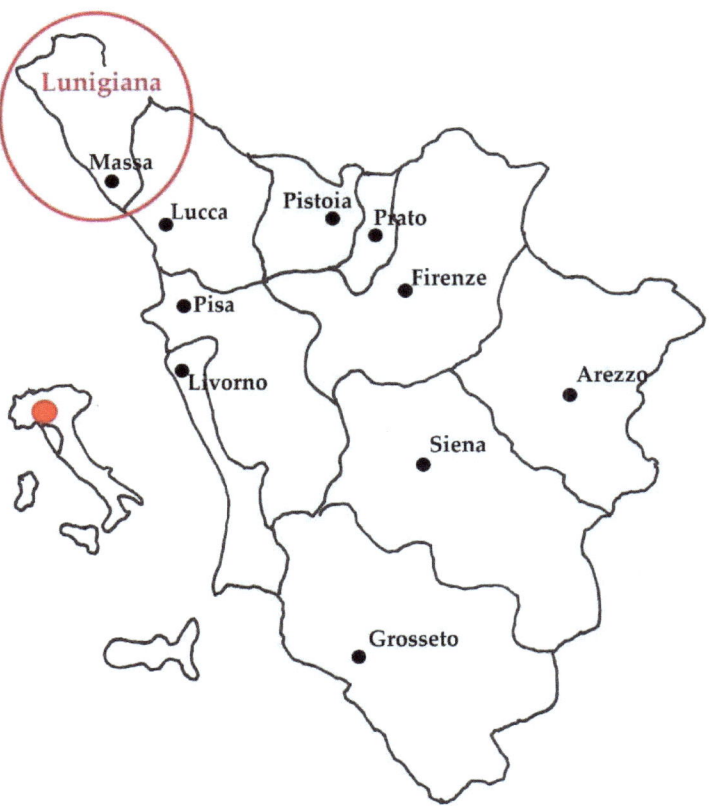

nature • culinary • culture

Imprint / legal notice

If you liked the book, just send me an e-mail stating the title to: post@lunigiana-toskana.de I look forward to hearing from you. You can always find more information and news at www.lunigiana-toskana.de

Bibliographic information of the German National Library: The German National Library lists this publication in the German National Bibliography; detailed bibliographic data is available on the Internet at http://dnb.dnb.de.
The automated analysis of the work in order to obtain information, in particular about patterns, trends and correlations in accordance with §44b UrhG ('Text and Data Mining') is prohibited.
© 2025 Dietmar W. Brandt
© Sketches, drawings and photographs Dietmar W. Brandt
Proofreading: Tom Orrow Glasgow Scotland
Other contributors: tutti gli amici della Lunigiana
Publisher: BoD · Books on Demand GmbH, Überseering 33, 22297 Hamburg, bod@bod.de
Printed by: Libri Plureos GmbH, Friedensallee 273, 22763 Hamburg
ISBN: 978-3-8192-2582-6

Per XVI IX LXX
incantavole
Mocron sempar pu blu

Content

Ti voglio tanto bene

When thinking of Tuscany, familiar images immediately appear before the mind's eye: endless cypress-lined avenues, gently rolling hills, golden wheat fields bathed in the warm evening light. The classic postcard idyll that has attracted visitors from all over the world for decades. But Tuscany has another, wilder, more mysterious side, one that is not found in well-manicured vineyards or picturesque Renaissance cities. A side hidden between the mountains and the sea, where the gentle curves of the landscape give way to rugged cliffs and dense forests of chestnut and oak. This region is different. Here, Tuscany is not golden but green and rocky. The peaks of the Apuan Alps rise sharply into the sky, while to the west, the Ligurian coast stretches out, where the sea glistens in the distance like a promised secret. Lunigiana is a land of castles, medieval villages, and hidden valleys. A region that does not loudly showcase its past but quietly preserves it within its weathered walls. Here, the wind sweeps through abandoned fortresses, ancient springs bubble along pilgrimage routes, while in the trattorias, steaming bowls of pasta and freshly grated pecorino are served. It is an undiscovered Tuscany, one that does not immediately reveal itself to everyone. It has nothing in common with the tourist clichés of Florence or Siena. Those who come here do not find a staged version of Italy but a real one. This book is an invitation. An invitation to get to know Lunigiana—its landscapes, its people, its cuisine and its soul. My stories are meant to inspire you to discover this gem in your own way and create lasting memories. Welcome to Lunigiana, my new home, which I have come to love so deeply.

Lunigiana—I am very fond of you! Ti voglio tanto bene.

Lunigiana with Alpi Apuane

Luni – the sunken city – the origin of Lunigiana

Before Lunigiana existed, before castles crowned the hills and pilgrims travelled through the valleys on the Via Francigena, there was a city that gave this region its name: Luni. Today, Luni is a quiet, almost unremarkable place, but once, it was one of the most important Roman colonies in northern Italy. A city of marble, wealthy, flourishing, and situated directly by the sea. A city visited by emperors, praised by poets and known by merchants around the world. Yet, like so many great places of antiquity, it slowly sank into oblivion. Its stones were plundered, its history buried beneath layers of earth. And yet, its name lives on, in Lunigiana, in the landscape and in the people who have made this region their home.

A city of marble and legends
Luni was founded in 177 BC by the Romans, following their victory over the Ligurian Apuani, who had ruled the land between the mountains and the sea until then. It was strategically located near the Tyrrhenian Sea, with direct access to the rivers and valleys of the Apennines. But what truly made Luni special was its marble. Just a few kilometres away, in the mountains of Carrara, the most famous marble of antiquity was quarried. The white marble of Luni was so pure and exquisite that it was exported throughout the Roman world. The Pantheon in Rome, the Forum, countless temples and villas were built from this prized stone. The city grew and thrived, becoming a centre of trade, a hub for merchants, sailors, and craftsmen. At its peak, Luni was home to more than 50,000 people—an enormous number for ancient times, making it the second-largest city after Rome.

Its streets were paved, it had temples, thermal baths, a vast forum and most impressively: an amphitheatre for over 7,000 spectators, the remains of which still stand today.

The Golden Age and the slow decline

But with fame came envy. Luni was attacked multiple times by pirates and barbarian invaders. By the 4th century, its decline had begun. The rivers silted up the harbours, the sea slowly receded and trade routes shifted. The once-proud city gradually disappeared into the swamps of history. By the Middle Ages, it was completely abandoned. Its stones were used to build villages in the surrounding area, its temples vanished. The people who settled further inland carried the name "Luni" with them and called the entire region: Lunigiana – the land of Luni.

A Walk through the past

Today, Luni is a place for explorers. No longer a grand city but an archaeological site where history and nature intertwine. A walk through the ruins takes visitors past the remains of the ancient forum, the foundations of villas and temples and finally to the impressive Roman amphitheatre, still preserved in its semi-circular form. Here, where gladiators once fought and actors performed tragedies, silence now reigns. The wind blows through the tall grass, cicadas sing and only a few visitors find their way here. But those who close their eyes can still imagine the city with marble-paved streets, where chariots once rolled, Dockworkers, trading with ships from Spain, Greece and Egypt. Merchants bringing exotic goods from across the Mediterranean and Patricians gazing out over the sea from their villas, believing their city would last forever. Luni may now lie in ruins, but its story lives on—in every stone of the region, in every name, in every memory. Without Luni, there would be no

Lunigiana. Without its past, there would be no castles, no medieval towns, no ancient pilgrimage routes telling the tale of a Roman city that once stood on the edge of the world. Yet was the vital centre of an entire region. A visit to Luni is not a typical Tuscany experience. There are no picture-perfect postcard views here, no tourist crowds, no stylish cafés, except for a small museum area. But there is the silence of history. And sometimes that is worth more than any post-card view.

amphitheatre of Luni

amphitheatre of Luni

museum in Luni

Pontremoli – the trembling bridge

There are times you never forget—times when the internet didn't yet rule the world, and travel recommendations came from real people, not from apps and algorithms. In hushed, conspiratorial tones, whispered secrets were shared about hidden restaurants, deserted side streets and picturesque places.

I had almost forgotten these good old days since moving to Lunigiana, until I was reminded of this lost tradition in my neighbouring town Pontremoli. This small town in northern Tuscany lies between two rivers, the Magra and the Fiume Verde. Its name comes from the Italian words *ponte* (bridge) and *tremare* (to tremble), making Pontremoli the "trembling" or "shaking bridge."

A spontaneous stop

On a sunny day in the 1990s, I was once again driving from Germany to La Spezia to visit my friends and business partners. I was cruising along the E33, which winds like a silver thread through the heart of Lunigiana. As I reached Pontremoli, I spontaneously decided to take a coffee break. I was tired from the monotonous highway drive and needed a rest. I left the E33 and took the SS62, heading straight into the town centre. There, I found a large free parking lot right by the Magra River. My first stop took me across the Ponte della Cresa, an old stone bridge connecting the two halves of the town. I paused for a moment, leaned against the cool stone and let my gaze wander: small boats bobbing on the river, colourful facades reflecting in the water, and somewhere in the distance, I heard the faint chime of a church bell. After crossing the medieval bridge, I suddenly found myself in the bustling Saturday morning market.

Feast for the senses

Market day in Pontremoli is a true feast for the senses. The market stretches across the small squares and winding streets of the old town. The air is filled with the aroma of fresh bread, aged cheeses, air-dried ham and sweet chestnut-based delicacies—all specialties of the region. I bought a piece of Parmesan and a Felino salami as a gift for my friends. Felino, the best salami in all of Italy.

As it is often the case in Italy, the market vendor immediately struck up a conversation, full of local tips. I just wanted a quick espresso, but she insisted, *"At this time of day, you should never drink coffee!"* I smiled puzzled. *"No, no, no!"* she exclaimed, gesturing animatedly, as my Italian was still quite basic at the time. *"You must go to Luciano's Bar in the Piazza. That's where the locals are having their aperitivo right now!"* Guess what I did?

Of course, I went to Luciano's Bar and ordered a Bianco Oro, an aperitivo made from a secret recipe by Roberto, the bar owner. He also informed me that one cannot leave Pontremoli without trying the famous Testaroli al Pesto, the signature dish of Lunigiana. Following his directions, I found the little Trattoria Norina, a cozy restaurant tucked away in one of the side alleys with a view of the Magra River.

Pontremoli

Unexpected culinary journey

As I enjoyed my Testaroli for lunch, I called Delisa and John to let them know I'd be late. Dear friends that moved from London to Italy, to enjoy the smallest village close to the riverbed of the Vara, the sister river of the Magra. *"Take your time, Dietmar,"* Delisa said warmly. *"And since you're in Pontremoli, you must go to the Swiss Café—they have incredible pastries!"* Naturally, I followed this advice too. Thanks to the many Swiss families who settled in Pontremoli in the 19th century to open cafés and patisseries, the town is still home to the famous Caffè degli Svizzeri on Piazza della Repubblica. This is where the famous "Amor" pastries were invented, small, delicious treats that have become a symbol of the town. These delicate pastries are made with a secret buttercream recipe sandwiched between two crispy wafers. Their size and shape resemble the well-known german Hanuta wafers.

Amor wafers

The Amor pastries turned out to be one of the best recommendations I had ever received. And the moment you taste them, you immediately understand why they bear that name. So, as you can read, it's always worth talking to locals at length and asking questions. And if you're still struggling with vocabulary, you can use your hands, feet or a piece of napkin for a quick sketch.

Glimpse on history

Pontremoli is more than just a town, it is a living history book. In the Middle Ages, it was a key stop on the Via Francigena, the famous pilgrimage route from Canterbury to Rome. Merchants, pilgrims, nobles, and warriors passed through these streets, and the traces of their stories are still visible today. I followed the main street and reached Piazza della Repubblica, the beating heart of Pontremoli.

Here, small cafés, boutiques, and bookstores line the square, a perfect blend of tradition and modern life. I took a moment to soak in the atmosphere before heading toward the town's landmark: The Castello del Piagnaro, the fortress towering over the town. The Castle above Pontremoli is one of the most fascinating towns in the region—a place so rich in history that you can almost hear its stories as you wander its streets. Towers rise above the rooftops, stone bridges span the Magra River and above it all, the Castello del Piagnaro stands majestically, guarding Pontremoli for centuries. The path to the castle leads through narrow, cobbled alleys, winding steeply uphill. Once at the top, the effort is rewarded: the view over the town and the surrounding green hills of Lunigiana is simply spectacular. The fortress itself is a blend of medieval architecture and modern museum exhibits. Inside is the Museo delle Statue Stele, which houses the mysterious stone statues found throughout Lunigiana. These ancient, human-like sculptures date back to the Bronze Age and remain an archaeological enigma. Who created them? What was their purpose? No one knows for sure, but that is precisely what makes them so magical. At the museum, you can admire these moon-shaped stone figures, whose age and origins still puzzle researchers. To date, around 80 of these statue or stele menhirs have been discovered in Lunigiana. Most of them were found in rural areas in pastures, at fords or on mountain passes. The first statue menhir was discovered in 1827 in the village of Nova in the municipality of Zignago in the province of La Spezia. In 1886, two small rectangular stelae were found underwater in the Gulf of La Spezia, but were lost. In 1905, nine buried statues were found in Fivizzano. The discovery was made by a farmer who found them lined up in a row, sorted by height and facing east. The stone statues from Pontevecchio are among the oldest finds. The most recent discoveries were made in 2005 in the municipality of Mulazzo. Inaugurated in 1975, the Museo delle statue stele lunigianesi (Museum of Statues Stelae) in the Castello del Piagnaro in Pontremoli collects all the statues in Lunigiana, both originals and copies. I run my fingers over the cold, smooth stone of one of the statues - a direct contact with the past. A moment of reverence. Another special testimony to the town's former wealth is the Villa Dosi Delfini.

To this day, the villa is used by the Dosi family as a temporary retreat from Milanese city life - and its prestigious status. Some of the rooms in the villa can be booked for weddings, but as you can imagine, this is not cheap. It is now also possible to book tickets online on the website and the associated calendar. You will then receive a personalised guided tour of the villa and the enchanting garden. Let yourself be surprised by the former influence and wealth of the Dosi in the baroque villa with its water and light effects and numerous trompe l'oeils. In the Palazzo Dosi Magnavacca in Pontremoli's old town, the splendour of the atrium, the main staircase and the grand hall, which is decorated with paintings and mythological stories, tells of the wealth and power of this immensely rich merchant family. The size of the palazzo gives a good idea of Pontremoli society in the 18th century, where the useful was combined with the pleasant and where art and culture were always closely intertwined with trade and commerce.

Pontremoli – the city of books

Back in the old town, I discovered why Pontremoli is also called "Città del Libro"—The City of Books. Every summer, the town hosts the Premio Bancarella, a prestigious Italian literary prize founded in the 1950s by traveling booksellers. The very first winner? Ernest Hemingway, with *The Old Man and the Sea*. As I wandered, I stumbled upon a charming little bookstore tucked inside a stone vault. The owner, an elderly gentleman with reading glasses, greeted me warmly and showed me some of his favourite books about Lunigiana. I flipped through old maps, admired beautifully bound volumes, and picked up a book about the history of Via Francigena—the perfect souvenir.

"Era entrata con piccoli passi esitanti, la prudenza dei bambini quando vogliono qualcosa. Appoggiata ad una valigia, s'era messa a fissarmi dondolando un piede su e giù. Fuori era novembre, il vento invernale, gelava i boschi della mia Toscana."

PREMIO BANCARELLA
1970
ORIANA FALLACI
"NIENTE E COSÌ SIA"

Pontremoli
Città del Libro

As I got back in my car and started the engine, I took one last look at the towers, the bridges, the narrow alleys before heading off to see my friends.

Pontremoli is not a town to rush through, it is a town to experience, to feel, to taste and to remember. It combines medieval charm with vibrant culture and traditional craftsmanship with culinary delights. Little did I know then that this region would one day become my new home.

Attenzione! Speed camera alert!

My road trip continues south on the SS62, but caution is advised: Italians are known for their politeness, especially when it comes to warning about speed cameras. On the short stretch from Pontremoli to Filattiera, just 12 kilometres and there are two of these well-calibrated traps lurking along the way. You can't even risk exceeding the limit by two kilometres per hour!

I can tell you from my experience: the speeding tickets didn't arrive promptly—they took their time, likely due to various bureaucratic delays. Sometimes, it took up to nine months before they finally arrived in Germany. There is a 46% discount if you pay within ten days, but even then, exceeding the speed limit by just two kilometres per hour still cost me 48 euros. So, my recommendation? Stick to the speed limits—it saves money.

Continuing towards Filattiera, you pass through the small, inconspicuous village of Scorcetoli.

The town even has its own railway station on the Parma–La Spezia line, though it's mostly abandoned. Train tickets can still be purchased from a Trenitalia vending machine. Apart from a small bar near the station, there isn't much to see here except for my personal trusted truffle dealer, "Lunigiana Tartufo da Simone Mori."

Lunigiana truffles

Diamonds of the local cuisine

Lunigiana's truffles are a rare and unique delicacy in the local cuisine. A few years ago, Simone Mori started his own business, building a small but refined truffle production company. He decided to create a range of jams, creams, seasonings, and other truffle-based delicacies, using primarily local raw ingredients grown or sourced directly in Lunigiana. This allows him to maintain a short supply chain, reducing unnecessary transport distances.

Simone focuses mainly on truffle-infused jams, combining flavours like onion, chestnut, potato, apple, pear, bell pepper, pumpkin and honey. A visit to his shop is absolutely worthwhile, especially since you can buy fresh seasonal truffles to elevate your homemade pasta dishes.

truffle jams

For a true culinary highlight, try fresh bread topped with fried eggs and truffle. It's a small but precious treasure that you simply cannot miss.

Filattiera – a village of history and indulgence

Nestled atop a serene hill overlooking the Magra Valley, the village of Filattiera stands as a testament to the rich tapestry of history woven through the Lunigiana region. Its origins trace back to the Bronze Age, with layers of epochs evident in the stones of its ancient houses. Walking through its narrow alleys, one can feel the whispers of time, each corner revealing a story from the past.

Crossroads of history

Filattiera's strategic location made it a significant stop along the Via Francigena, the ancient pilgrimage route stretching from Canterbury to Rome. Long before the Romans, the Ligurian Apuani settled in this area, leaving behind enigmatic stele statues, ancient stone sculptures with stylized faces and bodies, whose true meanings remain shrouded in mystery. These artifacts offer a glimpse into the early civilizations that once thrived here.

In the 13th century, the powerful Malaspina family recognized the village's strategic importance and constructed a castle to protect their territories. This fortress allowed them to oversee the entire Magra Valley and control the flow of travellers along the Via Francigena. Today, the Castello di Filattiera stands as a majestic reminder of the past, its walls echoing tales of battles, alliances and the ever-changing dynamics of power. A short distance from the castle lies the Pieve di Santo Stefano, a Romanesque church. Inside, visitors can find ancient stele statues, linking the site to the area's prehistoric roots.

History you can touch

Castello di Filattiera

Once an impregnable fortress of the Malaspina, today, parts of the walls and towers remain intact. From this elevated spot, you can enjoy a breathtaking view over the valley especially in the evening light, when the sun slowly sets behind the mountains, casting a golden glow over the landscape.

Pieve di Sorano

Apart from the hilltop village itself, one of the most significant historical landmarks in Filattiera is the Pieve di Sorano, a Romanesque parish church dating back to the 11th century. Located along the SS62, this church stands in an area where prehistoric settlements once thrived, as evidenced by the discovery of seven Stele Statues in Sorano, two of which are displayed on the church's facade. The Pieve di Sorano was likely the most important religious seat of the Diocese of Luni in Lunigiana. This large and well-preserved building sits at a key crossroad between northern and southern Italy. Its architectural features are also very unique, constructed from unpolished river stones, roofs made of slate, a distinct apse with three semi-circular sections, a square bell tower, making the church's silhouette unmistakable. The separate bell tower, possibly originally designed as a defensive structure, is connected to the church but is an independent element.

.

PIEVE DI SORANO 2024

L'Antica Pieve – the culinary gem

Filattiera would not be complete without a culinary recommendation. And in this small village, there is a place that offers exactly what you seek in Lunigiana: authentic, handmade food that makes time stand still. L'Antica Pieve is not just a restaurant—it is a piece of Filattiera itself. Located opposite the Pieve di Sorano, in an unremarkable modern building near a roundabout, this place might not look like much from the outside but inside, it is a hidden culinary treasure. The packed parking lot every lunchtime and evening hints at something special. The kind of place locals keep coming back to. The ground floor is underwhelming: a newsstand, a small but noisy bar and empty storefronts. But once you take the stairs or elevator to the first floor, everything changes. The warm aroma of fresh food and wood-fired pizzas greets you. Although the main dining area has the atmosphere of a train station hall, the heart of the place is Graziano, the owner, who creates a welcoming, cheerful ambiance. Together with his young and attentive team, Graziano ensures that guests feel at home, often stopping by tables for a friendly chat. The menu is well-balanced, offering a variety of local specialties including game, fish, mushrooms, and fresh vegetables, ensuring that even vegetarians find something to enjoy. But the true highlights of L'Antica Pieve are its exceptional wood-fired pizzas and pinse. Graziano even has two wood ovens, one in the main dining area and another for all the takeaway orders. The dough is perfect, with an incredible texture and the ingredients are always fresh. As for dessert, Graziano personally prepares it for each guest at a dedicated dessert bar in the dining room.

Tips for dining

Arrive between 7 and 8 pm to avoid the later Italian dinner rush. In summer, reserve a table on the terrace for a peaceful, scenic dining experience. This is not a fancy, pretentious place but rather a pure and authentic Italian dining experience. What to Order?

- Testaroli al pesto – Lunigiana's ancient pasta, made from wheat dough, cooked in cast-iron plates, and served with fresh pesto.
- Tagliatelle ai funghi porcini – Homemade pasta with porcini mushrooms from the surrounding forests, garnished with local truffles.
- Agnello al forno – Oven-roasted lamb with Lunigiana's wild herbs.

The wine list features not only local wines from Lunigiana and Liguria but also an excellent selection of Italian favourites. Dining here does not feel like eating in a restaurant, it feels like sitting in the large dining room of an Italian family, enjoying the best flavours the region has to offer. Filattiera is not a loud village. It does not seek attention, nor does it boast world-famous landmarks. But it has a soul. It is a place where you can feel the past, embrace the landscape, and discover the true cuisine of the region. Whether you're wandering through its narrow alleys, following the paths of pilgrims or simply sitting on the terrace of L'Antica Pieve with a glass of wine. Filattiera is a place that stays with you. A village you may stumble upon by chance while traveling toward the sea but one you'll always want to return to.

Bagnone – A gem in the heart of Lunigiana

The day begins, as it so often does here, with a light mist gently draping itself over the hills of Lunigiana like a delicate veil.
I drive along a winding country road, passing through a landscape so breathtakingly beautiful that it almost seems unreal: dense chestnut forests, babbling brooks and the occasional stone house, blending seamlessly into nature.
Today's destination: Bagnone, one of the most romantic villages in the region. The arrival in Bagnone – a picture-perfect village.

Bagnone

As I roll my Fiat 124 Spider over the cobbled piazza, I immediately feel that Bagnone is different: more enchanted, peaceful, almost poetic. The old stone houses nestle tightly together, as if warming each other. A medieval bridge stretches elegantly across the Bagnone River, whose crystal-clear waters meander through the village. I park at the edge of the historic centre and stroll in slowly. The narrow alleys, some covered by archways that create tunnel-like passages, exude an irresistible charm.

The air smells of wood fires, damp stone and history. Bagnone is not large, but that is exactly what makes it so captivating. It feels like stepping back in time into a world that has found its own rhythm.

The perfect viewpoint

My first stop takes me up to the Castle of Bagnone, which sits majestically above the village. The climb along the ancient, cobbled paths is steep, but every step is worth it. At the top, I am rewarded with a breathtaking view: Gentle green hills stretch endlessly toward the horizon, while below, the village wraps itself around the river like a postcard come to life. The castle itself is mostly in ruins today, yet its ancient tower still stands proudly, a silent witness to the centuries when Bagnone was a strategic stronghold along the old trade and pilgrimage routes. I linger for a while, taking in the scenery and enjoying the absolute serenity.

Coffee & stories on the Piazza

Back in the village, I head to the heart of Bagnone. The charming Piazza Roma, which sits directly by the river. Here, people gather on stone benches, chatting with neighbours or simply watching village life unfold. I order an espresso at the Bar del Borgo, a tiny, cozy café run by the same family for generations. Next to me, elderly gentlemen engage in animated debates about politics, while a Nonna offers her grandson a piece of cake. Life here is unhurried, authentic, and unfiltered, just like the complete Lunigiana itself.

Feast for the senses

Bagnone is best known for its agricultural heritage and deep-rooted connection to chestnut cultivation. For centuries, people here lived in the chestnut groves, relying on this humble nut for survival. And, of course, Bagnone is also famous for its cuisine: Erbadela, chestnut pattona, and Treschietto onions are just a few of the local specialties. As a passionate food lover and Italian cuisine enthusiast for over 50 years, I have to share my Bagnone insider tips with you!

Discovering "La Lina"

My first culinary experience in Bagnone was during the purchase of my house in Mocrone. Accompanied by Silvia, the energetic seller from Munich, we drove to Bagnone for lunch. *"It has to be La Lina!"* she insisted. We arrived around 1:30 pm, a bit late for lunch, but the host still found us a table, despite his wife's initial reluctance. A three-course meal for 15 euros—I was curious to see what awaited me. And let me tell you, it was simply sensational.

Friendship over food

Today, Valter (the owner), his wife Francesca, and their son Nicolo have become dear friends. Not every traditional Locanda in Lunigiana offers such a diverse selection of antipasti, featuring regional delicacies that you won't find anywhere else:

- Wild boar salami
- Chestnut cake with fresh ricotta
- Torte d'erbe (a savory herb pie)
- A fantastic onion tart, made with the flavourful Treschietto onions, which thrive in the local soil

Valter is also a skilled truffle hunter and has an impressive network of regional suppliers, sharing his impressive knowledge and passion with every guest.

Slow-Food treasure

Locanda La Lina has long been recognized by the Slow Food movement as one of the top three traditional osterie in Lunigiana.

While they do have a menu, I highly recommend listening to Nicolo and following his daily recommendations. You won't be disappointed! My personal favourite dish is without a doubt, Tagliatelle con tartufo—a perfect autumn dish made with fresh local truffles, golden olive oil and finely grated Parmesan. A dream on a plate!

Few words about the Slow-Food movement

The movement was founded in Italy in 1986 by Carlo Petrini, originally under the name 'Arcigola'. It emerged as a reaction to the increasing spread of fast-food chains and aimed to preserve and promote regional cuisine and local food traditions. Today it is active in over 160 countries and has numerous members worldwide. A central project of Slow Food is the 'Ark of Taste' (Italian: 'Arca del Gusto'), which was launched in 1996. The aim of this project is to identify and protect endangered foods, crop varieties and livestock breeds. The criteria for inclusion in the Ark of Flavour are. Endangerment: The product must be threatened in its existence. Quality: It should have a unique flavour quality. Significance: The product should have historical significance and be identity-forming for a region. Sustainability: The production should support the sustainable development of the region.

tagliatelle con tartufo

The atmosphere in La Lina is also a curious speciality. The morbid charm of a bygone Art Nouveau era, a piano with sheet music by Giacomo Puccini as decoration, the old oak sideboards on which Valter has placed the Italian wine delicacies, the charming, somewhat yellowed wallpaper and the pictures by regional artists on the wall give the restaurant a very special charm. Somehow it all fits together. I am totally amazed every time I visit and discover something new and surprising every time.

Salotto La Lina

Another tip is to visit the small bar on the forecourt of La Lina before dinner. If you want to have an exotic drink beforehand or just a great aperitivo, there is a great bar just a few steps away from the entrance to La Lina in the same piazza, the Caffè Marconi - 'Baretto'.

Apricena is still celebrated here. Your drinks are accompanied by a small antipasto platter that is second to none. Buon appetito!

Pure nature

After dinner, I always wander down to the Bagnone River. The water is crystal clear, cascading over small waterfalls into natural pools. I follow the riverbank, listening to the gentle rush of water and the chorus of cicadas. Bagnone feels like a place where time has simply stopped. And this is such a splendid, longlasting experience.

"Bagnone is not just a place – it is something very special.
" *Whoever visits once will always return,"* the locals tell me. " *Eh, Sì, eh..."* I nod and smile, because at this moment, I understand exactly what they mean. A truly magical village. With wonderful people.

Villafranca in Lunigiana – my new home

There are places that touch you in a special way from the very beginning. Places that do not impose themselves on you, but rather quietly embrace and welcome you. For me, Villafranca in Lunigiana is exactly such a place. I still remember my first drive to Mocrone, a picturesque village of Villafranca. *"In winter, Mocrone has 100 residents; in summer 800,"* the locals say. Many city dwellers from Milan, Torino and Bergamo have holiday homes here, escaping the summer heat of the big cities.

My first encounter

Lois, the English real-estate agent, was driving ahead at quite a pace. After the first tight curves on the main road, I had already lost sight of her. Shortly after a small piazza at the village entrance, I suddenly encountered an S-shaped narrowing of the road. The passage between the old stone houses was so narrow that I abruptly hit the brakes and came to a stop. After a brief moment of shock, I carefully steered my car through the passage, while the sun cast long shadows across the tight alleyway. For an Ape, a Fiat 500, or a Vespa, this would have been no problem. But for a modern car with today's dimensions and endlessly beeping parking sensors, it was quite a challenge especially when facing it unexpectedly for the first time. Much later, after I had already moved here, I measured the passage for fun: The narrowest point is just 2.05 meters wide! By now, I can drive through it blindfolded except when another car suddenly appears coming the other way. That's when you witness my true italian driving skills in manoeuvring and reversing.

Since buying my house in 2022, this has become my home. The municipality of Villafranca in Lunigiana or simply Villafranca, as the locals call it. It is one of the most densely populated centres in the region. The Magra River flows gently through the valley, while history looms above it all. A history that lives on in the medieval walls, the weathered stones of castle ruins and in the faces of the people. Villafranca is not a town that demands attention. It is authentic, grounded and steeped in history that I discover and love a little more each day. Even the name itself reveals something about its past: "Villa Franca" – The Free Village.

Villafranca's place in history
In the Middle Ages, Villafranca was an important stop on the Via Francigena, the ancient pilgrimage route from Canterbury to Rome. Merchants, pilgrims, nobles, and travellers rested here before continuing their arduous journey. It's no surprise that the Malaspina family, one of the most powerful noble dynasties in northern Italy, also left their mark here. They built castles, fortified the area and controlled the trade routes that wound through the Magra Valley. Though these times have long since passed, the medieval charm still lingers over the town.

VILAFRANCA ... (signature) 2023

Things to see

Villafranca has more to offer than one might expect at first glance. For those who walk through the village with open eyes, history reveals itself in every corner.

The forgotten fortress

By the riverbank, the ruins of Castello di Malnido rise, a once mighty fortress of the Malaspina. Built in the 13th century, this fortress served as both a defensive outpost and a trade control point. Today, only ruins remain, yet standing there, it's easy to imagine knights patrolling the walls, merchants passing through the gates and pilgrims seeking refuge under the castle's protection.

Chiesa dei Santi Giovanni e Nicolo

Historic village centre & ancient bridges

A stroll through Villafranca takes you along narrow, cobbled streets, past centuries-old stone houses and across small bridges spanning the Magra River. One of the most impressive sights is the Ponte sul Magra, an ancient stone bridge that has withstood the test of time for centuries. At Piazza San Nicolo, you'll also find an exquisitely crafted marble sculpture of Dante Alighieri. Villafranca is not a flashy town. It doesn't have famous tourist attractions or grand landmarks. But it has something even more valuable: a soul. It's a place where history is alive, where the landscape invites exploration and where authentic italian life thrives. Whether you're wandering through the medieval alleys, crossing ancient bridges or simply watching the river flow beneath the castle ruins. Villafranca is a place that slowly but surely captivates your heart. And for me it has become home.

sculpture of Dante on Piazza San Nicolo

My culinary neighbour

Villafranca is not just history, it is also flavour, indulgence and hospitality. And I find all of this right across from my house—at Locanda Gavarini, in Mocrone. This restaurant is a true hidden gem, one of those places where you immediately feel welcome. The interior is unpretentious and warm, without unnecessary frills, exactly what a good ristorante should be. In summer, guests can enjoy large, covered terraces and spacious garden areas. An excellent swimming pool and an old wood-fired pizza oven complete the outdoor setting. It's no surprise that many weddings are celebrated here on mild summer nights. For those who want to stay longer, a few beautifully furnished rooms are also available. But what truly matters is the food and the atmosphere. And here this means pure Lunigiana gold.

Gavarini restaurant

What makes Gavarini so special?

Gavarini terrace

Home-made Pasta, just as It should be and you dreamed of:
- Gnocchi di funghi porcini su fonduta di Parmigiano al pro-
fumo di sottobosco

  *(porcini mushroom gnocchi in a Parmesan fondue with a
  woodland aroma)*
- Tagliolini fatti in casa al tartufo nero estivo e grattugiata di
uovo marinato

  *(hand-rolled tagliolini with summer black truffle and grated
  marinated egg—soft, delicate, and perfect)*
- Ravioli ripieni di carne e verdure, fatti in casa, con ragù alla
bolognese

  *(homemade ravioli stuffed with meat and vegetables,
  served with a classic bolognese ragù)*

Meat that melts in your mouth
- Bistecca alla Fiorentina

(A Florentine steak—crispy on the outside, butter-soft on the inside)

- Rollè di coniglio ripieno di castagne, servito con il suo fondo Aromatizzato e fichi caramellati
  (rolled rabbit stuffed with chestnuts, served with its own aromatic reduction and caramelized figs)

Desserts that tastes like home

- Mantecato alla crema con rum
  (A silky, rum-infused cream dessert)
- Babbà al rum con crema pasticcera
  (traditional rum-soaked sponge cake with pastry cream)

And then of course, there's the wine. The selection in Fabio's generously stocked wine cellar is outstanding, offering both regional and international wines from Vermentino and Canaiolo to the powerful reds from the Tuscan hills. Dining at Gavarini is not about pretentious fine dining. It's about honest, hearty cuisine, cooked with love since generations.

Feeling home in Lunigiana

There are many beautiful places in Lunigiana. But for me, Villafranca is something truly special. Maybe it's the history that lives within its ancient walls. Maybe it's the people, who greet you warmly, even if they've only known you for a few weeks. Maybe it's the food, which is as genuine as the region itself. Or maybe it's simply because with new friends by my side, I finally feel that I have arrived. And that is what makes this place my new home.

Mocrone

Virgoletta – a hidden gem

Just a few kilometres from Villafranca in Lunigiana, nestled among gentle hills and dense chestnut forests lies Virgoletta, a village that looks as if it has stepped straight out of a medieval painting.
With its winding alleys, closely packed stone houses and the imposing castle that watches over the village. Virgoletta is one of those hidden jewels that you don't stumble upon by accident. Those who come here seek authenticity, the untouched, original essence of Lunigiana, just as it once was and still is.

Fortified village
The name Virgoletta likely derives from the Latin word "virga", meaning "twig" or "small branch". Perhaps this refers to the lush forests surrounding the village, or to the ancient Ligurians, who settled here long before the Romans. Virgoletta is first mentioned in medieval documents, when it became an important fortified village at the border of the Malaspina territories. Like many places in Lunigiana, Virgoletta occupied a strategically significant location, close to the Via Francigena, but also in the crossfire of noble families vying for control over the region. During the 13th and 14th centuries, the village underwent major fortifications. A massive castle, thick stone walls, and narrow, defensible alleyways still bear witness to its turbulent past. Yet despite conquests, battles, and shifting rulers, Virgoletta endured, a silent guardian of history over the centuries.

Living history
From the moment you step into Virgoletta, you feel transported to another era. The narrow, cobbled streets wind through the village, so tight in places that the houses on either side seem to touch.

The first sight to catch your eye is the castle, standing proudly above the village. Originally built by the Malaspina, the fortress was later expanded and renovated by various noble families. Today it is not open to the public, but its mighty walls and towers still tell the tale of its former grandeur.

The Parish Church of San Lorenzo

At the heart of the village stands the Chiesa di San Lorenzo, a simple yet beautiful church dating back to the 12th century. Inside, you'll find impressive frescoes and an ornate marble altar, a testament to Virgoletta's deep-rooted religious traditions.

Old town walls & the gate to the past

Parts of the old village walls are still visible, once serving as a protective shield against invaders. Passing through the main gate, you almost feel like a medieval pilgrim, arriving in Virgoletta in search of rest and shelter. Though Virgoletta is today a small village with just a few hundred residents, it has preserved its strong identity. It is a place for explorers, for lovers of hidden gems and for those seeking authenticity. A walk through Virgoletta is a journey into the past but also a glimpse into a way of life that has nearly vanished in the modern world. Here, there is no rush, no noise, only the silence of history and the warmth of its people. Perhaps that is the true secret of Lunigiana.

Virgoletta streets

Mulazzo – the village of the Malaspina

Mulazzo is one of those villages that feels like a storybook from a bygone era. Perched high on a hill, surrounded by olive groves and chestnut forests and overlooking the Magra Valley, this small village in Lunigiana has a history far greater than its size. Here, among the ancient castle ruins and winding alleys, history was written by nobles, scholars and pioneers who shaped Lunigiana. And that is why Mulazzo is not just a beautiful place, but a treasure trove of the past, whose secrets remain alive to this day.

Strategic centre of the Lunigiana

The history of Mulazzo is closely tied to the powerful Malaspina family, who ruled over Lunigiana for centuries. As early as the 12th century, the Malaspina built a fortress here to control the trade routes through the Magra Valley and secure their influence. Mulazzo was not just a border town between the different Malaspina territories, but also a political and cultural hub. As one of the most important strongholds in the region, it was the stage for intrigues, power struggles and alliances. Even today, the ruins of Mulazzo Castle tell the tale of this eventful past. Its ancient walls, once home to kings and knights, still gaze over the valley. Silent witnesses to the power that once reigned here.

Village of poets and explorers
But Mulazzo is more than a place of castles and battles. It is a village that has shaped literature and exploration.

Home of Alessandro Malaspina – the tuscan Magellan
Mulazzo's most famous son is Alessandro Malaspina, a nobleman and explorer who in the 18th century, travelled the world. He led one of the largest scientific expeditions for the Spanish crown, charting new trade routes, mapping coastlines and studying foreign cultures. His journey took him to South America, Alaska, the Philippines and Australia, yet his roots always remained in Mulazzo. Today, a small museum in the village is dedicated to him, displaying maps, journals and artifacts from his travels.

Village of books
Mulazzo is also known as "Borgo dei Libri"—the village of books. Every year it hosts the "Selvaggio West" festival, dedicated to literature, travel and discovery. A tribute to Alessandro Malaspina and his adventurous spirit. Numerous small bookstores, literary walks and events keep the tradition of knowledge and storytelling alive in this historic village.

Things to see

A walk through Mulazzo feels like a journey through time. The narrow alleys, ancient stone houses and unexpected panoramic views. Everything here tells a story. The heart of Mulazzo is its old castle, once the centre of Malaspina rule. Though only parts of the walls and towers remain today, the sense of power and history is still palpable. From the castle ruins, the view over the Magra Valley is spectacular. A scene once enjoyed by the nobles of the past.

Torre di Dante – a myth?

An ancient tower in Mulazzo is rumoured to have sheltered Dante Alighieri during his exile in Lunigiana. Whether it is true or not, the legend adds even more to its mystique.

The Malaspina museum

For those interested in the history of Lunigiana's most influential family, this small museum is a must-visit. It showcases the Malaspina dynasty's legacy and artifacts from their rule.

Admission: €6 (Open from June 15 – September 30).

Mulazzo – A village that lives on

Mulazzo may be small, but it has a fantastic history. Summer festivals, book fairs and wine tastings bring the village to life. Mulazzo is not a place to simply pass through, it is a place to experience. A lovely piece of Lunigiana, rewarding those who dare to wander off the beaten path.

Aulla – between history, destruction and rebirth

The SS 62 road to Aulla takes me through a landscape that gently transitions into the rolling hills of Lunigiana. While the neighbouring villages often feel secluded and almost enchanted, Aulla tells a different story, a story of war, rebuilding, and transformation. The moment I arrive, it's clear: Aulla is different. It's not like the medieval, romantic Pontremoli or the dreamy Bagnone. Life here is busier, more modern. Yet behind its contemporary facades lies a past deeply rooted in Lunigiana's history.

Abbey of San Caprasio – the spiritual heart

My first stop is the Abbazia di San Caprasio, one of the oldest religious buildings in Lunigiana. Built as early as the 9th century, it served as a crucial resting place for pilgrims traveling along the Via Francigena. As soon as I step inside, I am enveloped in a profound silence, almost tangible. The thick stone walls whisper of a time when monks offered shelter and refuge to weary travellers. Today, the abbey houses a small yet fascinating archaeological museum, bringing the history of the region to life. One of the most impressive exhibits is the recently discovered medieval crypt and ancient burial sites, only uncovered a few years ago. I let my gaze wander over the old walls and imagine the past, the weary pilgrims, the travellers seeking rest, the monks in silent prayer.

Most iconic landmark

From the abbey, I make my way to Aulla's most famous site: The Fortezza della Brunella. Perched high above the town, this 16th-century fortress offers a breathtaking panoramic view over the Magra Valley. Originally built by the Medici to control this strategically vital region, its massive walls have withstood wars, sieges and natural disasters. But what fascinates me most about this fortress is not just its military history, but a very special resident: Kinta Beevor. Kinta was the daughter of Aubrey Waterfield, a British painter who fell in love with the Lunigiana and made the fortress his home. Here, within these rugged, historic walls, Kinta spent part of her childhood, surrounded by art, nature and the charm of a bygone era. In her book "A Tuscan Childhood", she reminisces about her time in Lunigiana—the castle gardens, the endless summers and encounters with locals. Her memories paint a vivid, almost magical picture of life in a British artist's household in Italy at the start of the 20th century.

Fortress with centuries of history

Aubrey Waterfield, one of England's most notable painters, married Caroline Lucie Isabella Jane Duff Gordon (also known as Lina Duff Gordon) in 1902—a historian and journalist for *The Observer*, and co-founder of the British Institute of Florence. Together with their two sons, Gordon and John and their daughter Kinta, they moved to Italy. In 1920, Waterfield first rented, then purchased the Fortezza della Brunella, where he painted remarkable portraits, landscapes and floral scenes inspired by Lunigiana. The fortress itself is the most imposing in all of Lunigiana. Built during the Renaissance, it dominates the rocky cliffs above Aulla, controlling the main trade routes of the region. While historical sources rarely mention the fortress, the first known record dates to 1553, suggesting it was already operational by that time. Historians debate its origin, it may have been built by Giovanni dalle Bande Nere (who acquired Aulla in 1523 from the Malaspina di Lusuolo), then Jacopo Ambrogio Malaspina (who ruled Aulla in the late 15th century), or Adamo Centurione, a Genoese noble who took control of Aulla in 1543. After the 18th century, the Centurione family lost the fortress to the

Malaspina, and in 1860, it passed into private ownership. In 1920, the Waterfield family restored it, before selling it to the Italian state in 1977. Today, it is open to visitors on certain days and houses the Natural History Museum of Lunigiana, featuring four exhibition halls exploring the region's geological and ecological history.

Moment of reflection

On this beautiful July day, I sit on the stone walls of the fortress, gazing over the Magra Valley. Maybe Kinta once sat here too, looking into the distance, dreaming about her future not knowing that years later, she would share her memories of this castle with the world. Now, I wish to do the same to share the beauty of this region with you.

Market life & culinary discoveries

Every Saturday, Aulla transforms into a vibrant market scene filled with fresh vegetables, fragrant herbs, homemade cheeses and spicy cured meats. One particular stand catches my eye: A vendor selling Lunigiana honey, a true regional delicacy. Locals swear by its intense flavour, especially the chestnut honey, which has a slightly bitter note. Next to it, a freshly baked focaccia, drizzled with olive oil and still warm from the oven. I can't resist to buy a piece and take a bite.

Town of change

Aulla has seen its share of hardships. Unlike other towns in Lunigiana that have preserved their medieval charm. Aulla was heavily bombed during World War II. Much of its historic architecture was lost forever. But the city rose again, reinventing itself into a lively, dynamic place. Here, history meets the present, streets bustle with life, young people sit in cafés, shops are busy, yet the echoes of the past linger in every corner.

"Per Bacco"

Some restaurants you visit, enjoy, pay for and forget. And then there are places like "Per Bacco". Places that leave a lasting imprint on your memory. From the moment you step inside, you realize this is more than just a restaurant. The warm stone walls, the inviting terrace overlooking the piazza, the soft lighting, the shelves lined with fine wines, an atmosphere that blends elegance with genuine italian warmth.

What to Order? Start with an antipasti platter, showcasing the best of Lunigiana:

- Lardo di colonnata, melting like butter on your tongue
- Pecorino with chestnut honey, a perfect balance of savoury and sweet
- Homemade crostini with chicken liver pâté, creamy, rich, and perfectly seasoned

For the main course:
- Tagliolini alla salvia—fresh pasta with butter, sage, and freshly shaved truffles
- Brasato al Chianti—beef braised for hours in Chianti wine, served with velvety mashed potatoes

And for dessert:
- Torta di Ricotta e Pere—a fluffy ricotta-pear cake, just sweet enough

"Per Bacco" is not just a simple restaurant. It is a love letter to tuscan cuisine. Every dish, every detail, every glass of wine is carefully chosen. You don't just eat here, you experience a memorable evening. And I will certainly be coming back.

1 Ernährung bei Verbrennungen

Diese Empfehlungen bitte immer mit Ernährungsberater/in, Arzt oder Diätologen/in absprechen! Die Rezepte und Zutatenlisten unterstützen die medizinischen Therapien.

Die Kalorienangaben frischer Zutaten (Obst und Gemüse) und die Inhaltsstoffe schwanken je nach Qualität und Erntezeit. Die Inhalte wurden von einer Diätologin und einer Ernährungsberaterin für die Traditionelle Chinesische Medizin (TCM) geprüft.

Autor:
©2022 Josef Miligui
Liebe Leserinnen und Leser, ich wünsche Ihnen viel Erfolg und gutes Gelingen bei der Umstellung Ihrer Ernährung. Dieses Buch wurde aus eigener Erfahrung mit Krankheit und Ernährung geschrieben und ich habe schon immer das Zubereiten guter Speisen geschätzt. Wenn Sie nicht so geübt sind im Kochen, empfiehlt sich ein Kurs bei Ernährungsberatern oder Diätologen, die Ihnen die Grundlagen der Kochmethoden sowie die richtige Verarbeitung der Zutaten vermitteln können. Anhand der Lebensmittellisten aus diesem Buch können Sie weitere Rezepte entwickeln und entdecken.

Quelle:
Die Listen werden aus der EBNS-Datenbank für die Ernährungsberatung generiert. Die Datenbank wird von Ernährungsberater, Therapeuten und Ärzte für die Beratung der Patienten/Klienten verwendet und ermöglicht eine Kombination mehrerer Syndrome.

Literaturliste:
Wir haben die Unterlagen als Wissensbasis genutzt und an unsere Erfahrungen angepasst und ergänzt.
www.ebns.at

Herstellung und Verlag:
BoD – Books on Demand, Norderstedt
ISBN: 9783837065572

DIÄTETIK - veränderter Nährstoffbedarf - nach Verbrennungen
(Buch: 050)

1.1 Vorwort

Die Weltgesundheitsorganisation (WHO) davon spricht, dass bis zu 80% der Erkrankungen durch äußere Faktoren wie Ernährung, Lebensstil, Umweltgifte und dergleichen beeinflusst werden.

Welche Faktoren also jeder einzelne von uns aktiv beeinflussen kann und somit seine Chancen auf Erhöhung der allgemein Gesundheit erzielen kann, darum geht es auf den folgenden Seiten.

Der Fokus in diesem Buch liegt auf dem Faktor mit der größten Hebelwirkung - der Ernährung.
Schon Hippokrates hat einst gesagt "Lass die Nahrung deine Medizin sein und Medizin deine Nahrung!" Kräuterpädagog:innen heute sagen so: "Es gibt für jede Krankheit das richtige Kraut."

Egal wie wir es drehen und wenden, wir sind was wir essen (und was unser Essen gegessen hat). Der moderne Mensch sieht sich gerne isoliert von seiner Umwelt. Wir entstehen aus unserer Umwelt, wir leben inmitten von ihr und wenn wir sterben gehen wir wieder in unsere Umwelt über. Während wir leben essen wir das, was in unserer Umwelt wächst (oder in Fabriken chemisch erzeugt wird). Diese Nahrung liefert die Energie und Bausteine, für den eigenen Körper, für den Stoffwechsel, Zellerneuerung, den Hormonhaushalt und damit für unser gesamtes Sein, die Gesundheit und unser Empfinden.

Hier ein paar Grundbausteine, bevor in dem Buch noch näher auf Ernährungsfaktoren eingegangen wird, die sozusagen der kleinste gemeinsame Nenner der meisten Ernährungsphilosophien sind: